P9-CNB-836

Erica Wilson The Craft of
Crewel Embroidery

Illustrated with drawings by
VLADIMIR KAGAN

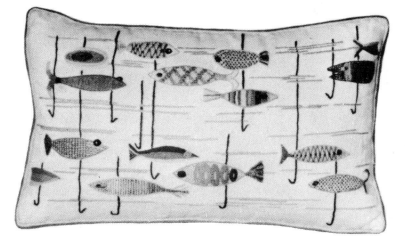

AND WITH PHOTOGRAPHS

Charles Scribner's Sons   *New York*

Abridgement
Copyright © 1971 Erica Wilson Kagan

Abridged from *Crewel Embroidery* by Erica Wilson.
Copyright © 1962 Erica Wilson Kagan.

Cover embroidery design, "Peaceful Woodland" © 1970 Erica Wilson

PICTURE CREDITS

Photos, Courtesy Victoria and Albert Museum, Crown Copyright: pages 35, 43, 87; courtesy Museum of Fine Arts, Boston: page 27; courtesy The Metropolitan Museum of Art, Rogers Fund, page 55; Hans Van Nes Studio: pages 1, 4, 13, 18, 24, 28, 30, 32, 39, 66; Chris Corpus: pages 38, 8, 81, 82; John R. Freeman & Co., London: pages 9, 11, 43, 87.

Designs, by the author: pages 1, 4 (adapted from a design in the Shelburne Museum), 9, 11, 13, 18, 24, 28, 30, 32, 38, 39, 81, 82; from patterns in the Victoria and Albert Museum: page 34.

Embroidery worked by Mrs. E. Farrar Bateson, page 39 (right); Mrs. Norman P. Clement, Jr., page 32 (bottom); Mrs. Eugene Geddes, page 1; Mrs. William F. LaPorte, Jr., page 13 (top); Mrs. Randall J. LeBoeuf, Jr., page 28; Mrs. Barent Lefferts, pages 4, 38; Mrs. Hampton S. Lynch, page 32 (top); Mrs. John B. Marsh, page 13 (bottom); Mrs. Grover O'Neill, page 18; Miss Louise E. Opitz, page 39 (left); Mrs. F. C. Windisch, page 30; the author, pages 9, 11, 24, 66 (courtesy of the Royal School of Needlework), 81, 82.

This book published simultaneously in the United States of America and in Canada—Copyright under the Berne Convention

All rights reserved. No part of this book may be reproduced in any form without the permission of Charles Scribner's Sons.

D-6.72[M]

Printed in the United States of America

SBN 684-12501-3 (Trade Paper, SL)

Contents

The free adaptation of an early American design for this screen lent itself to a great variety of stitches on a bold scale. The baskets were first worked on canvas and then appliquéed to the fabric.

Introduction

What is Crewel Work? The answer is simple. It is embroidery on practically any fabric in wool: a firm, two-ply variety known as "crewel" which really gives the needlework its name. With these quite limited means, and a battery of stitches at her command, the embroiderer today will find the possibilities for individual creation innumerable. Since the background is complete before the stitching is begun, crewel work is quick – in keeping with today's pace of living. But more important, the time can be as gaily spent producing a bed-spread as an eye-glass case, for the great variations possible in design, and the changing effect of color and stitch, make the work all-absorbing.

Crewel Work was most usually done for bed-spreads, valances and curtains for four-poster beds, wall hangings, pockets, (two of which would be tied round the waist, under a dress), and petticoats. Examples of all these have been found nowadays, so obviously they were the most popular articles for wool embroidery, though other items, such as chair seats or curtains, may well have been worked in crewels but have long since worn out owing to their practical nature. Historically, Crewel Work reached its peak in 17th century England and 18th century America.

During the nineteenth century Crewel Work fell victim to the Industrial Revolution. The advent of roller printing and cheap woven fabrics ended the need for decoration by embroidery – and Crewel Work became a lost art.

Happily today, Crewel Embroidery is experiencing a great revival, partly due to the interest in restoration, but especially to the American woman's desire to work with her hands. She has rediscovered the joy of creating embroidery that is individual and imaginative, and like her forebears will produce heirlooms for future generations.

To Begin

You want to learn to do Crewel Embroidery. Perhaps you have a definite idea of what you want to make. You have an eighteenth century love seat which you have been wanting to cover for years. Or a set of dining room chairs which would be charming in a crewel work design that echoes the chintz of the dining room curtains. Or you have seen and admired a friend's cashmere sweater which you were certain came from Paris, only to be told she had embroidered it herself. Or perhaps you have simple modern furniture and want a set of throw pillows in brilliant colors and heavy wools. Last but not least, perhaps you just want to learn embroidery for fun, and look forward to spending absorbing hours with a new hobby. Whichever way it is — the best way is to start by making a sampler.

A bedspread could be worked in squares and joined together afterward. Opposite: a French chair calls for a light design; a flowering tree design would be suitable for an English wing chair.

Start by Making a Sampler

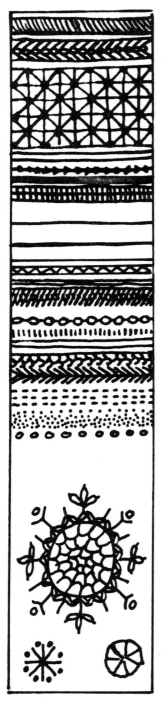

The word sampler came originally from the Latin word "Exemplar," to show, and that is exactly what it is. In this book you will find instructions for doing 47 stitches. Each one of these stitches may be varied in many ways by working with heavy or fine thread, by embroidering the stitches open or closely together and of course by changing color. So it is a good idea to have samples of some of these variations all on one strip of fabric. Then you may refer to it from time to time, just like a recipe book, when you are working on a specific project and trying to decide which stitch to put where.

To make a sampler, all you need are a few crewel wools, some embroidery needles, possibly a ring frame,* and last but not least, the material. A half a yard of linen is fine. This is best to practice on if it is closely woven, so you can't do better than buy linen twill, or a piece of ordinary pillow ticking. Because of the diagonal weave both are very firm materials and your stitches will be neat and clear. In the case of the ticking you can use the stripes as part of the design too.

The stitches used on the child's jacket (see page 11) are:

Braid	Satin (slanting)
Buttonhole	Rope
Cretan (open)	Roumanian
Roumanian	Split Stitch (worked in close rows)
Chain (worked as a wavy line)	Interlaced Herringbone
Fishbone (open)	Cable Chain
Herringbone	Seeding Straight Stitch
French Knots	Spider's Webs (woven)
Ziz-zag Chain	Buttonhole (2 rows back to back)

Using simple materials such as linen twill or ticking is really the best way at first.

* See Page 31 Wools and Needles; also see Page 26 Color. Page 20 Frames

Choosing Fabrics

FOR CHAIR SEATS, FOOTSTOOLS, WING ARMCHAIRS, ETC.

Use linen twill, closely woven worsted or wool tweed, or any material which is closely woven and not too variegated in texture to interfere with the embroidery. Material should be very strong for anything which is to receive wear and which is tightly stretched over a foundation, so be careful of some weaves which include synthetics – as some of these might not have the same durability as natural fibers.

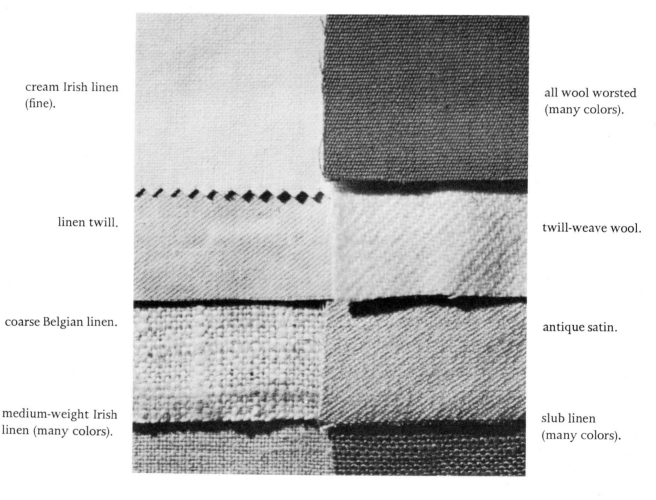

cream Irish linen (fine).

all wool worsted (many colors).

linen twill.

twill-weave wool.

coarse Belgian linen.

antique satin.

medium-weight Irish linen (many colors).

slub linen (many colors).

Child's jacket worked on ticking; the stitches used are listed on page 8.

FOR CURTAINS, BED-SPREADS, ETC.
(where the material will hang loosely)

Use Irish linen, homespun or hand-woven linen (if obtainable), antique satin or linen twill. Cotton or silk fabrics (unless mixed with other fibers) are generally too closely woven for the thickness of the wool – the needle will not draw through easily and the material will pucker.

FOR WALL HANGINGS, MIRROR FRAMES, PICTURES

Use any of the above materials, plus burlap, or any of the new "mixtures." Here the choice is much freer as the article will not receive hard wear.

Having obtained a simple ½ yd. of fabric for your sampler, however, the next stage is to begin the design.

Beginning the Design

If you commence with a sampler, it is best to work it in a design of some form, so that you can practice fitting the stitches into different shapes. Every moment is valuable, so it seems a pity to waste time on an embroidery which will lie in a drawer afterwards. Aim at making it into something you could use – a pillow, a telephone book cover – or plan it like one of the long strip samplers of the eighteenth century – adding things as you go along. Then you may even want to hang it on the wall afterwards!

Sketch out your pattern on "Layout" paper. The latter is better than tracing paper because it is heavier and yet you can see well enough to trace through it. A pad of it is obtainable from most art stores in all sizes. The largest made will be the most practical.

Divide the material in the simplest way possible so that the stitches can be varied without making the whole design confused. One idea is to draw a few basic lines, in a random pattern, then work out the rest as you go along, being guided by the stitches themselves. Otherwise you can make a geometric design which will give you practice at finding similar stitches to balance one another at opposite sides. Still another idea is to work the sampler in two halves, with all the close solid stitches on one side and the open ones on the other. Pillow ticking is of course the simplest of all, for within the restrictions of narrow banding you can use any stitches you choose. Having settled the form your sampler is to take, the next stage will consist of applying the pattern.

This tree makes a good sampler as the leaves and fruits are worked with many variations of solid filling stitches, sufficiently alike not to detract from the balance of the whole design.

A contemporary adaptation of the Elizabethan scrolling pattern, using the fruits of New York State instead of traditional flowers. Close solid stitches make it practical for the hard wear of a stool seat.

Applying the Pattern

There are several good ways of doing this. The first and easiest way is by

USING DRESSMAKERS' CARBON

Buy a packet of dressmakers' carbon from any notion department or sewing supply shop. (Ordinary carbon will smudge.) Fold the material in half and then half again, and crease the folds so that they show clearly. If the material happens to be crease-resistant, baste the center lines in both directions with a contrasting color thread. Then smooth the material flat on a table or board and hold it down evenly with masking tape on all four sides (as shown). A really smooth hard surface is necessary.

Fold the design, too, into four equal parts, and lay it down, still folded, so that it fits into one quarter of the fabric (as shown). Without shifting the paper, carefully unfold the design. The folds marking the center of the material and the paper will now be as one, and you will know the design is placed exactly in the middle. (Of course you must be sure your design was in the center of the folded paper first!)

Now slide a sheet of carbon paper, face downwards, between paper and material. Use blue carbon for light materials, white for dark ones. Anchor the paper with some heavy weights (books, paperweights, etc.) and trace round the outline *very heavily* with a pencil. Using weights is a better idea than taping the design all round, because you can lift a corner occasionally to see how well the carbon is transferring. You really must *engrave* heavily to get good results, but you will soon find this out as you work.

The two drawbacks to this method are: (1) The design is often spoiled by the heavy pencil marks, and (2) Some materials will not take the carbon easily. Therefore, especially when the design is to be used more than once, there is no more accurate method of transferring a design than by making a pricking.

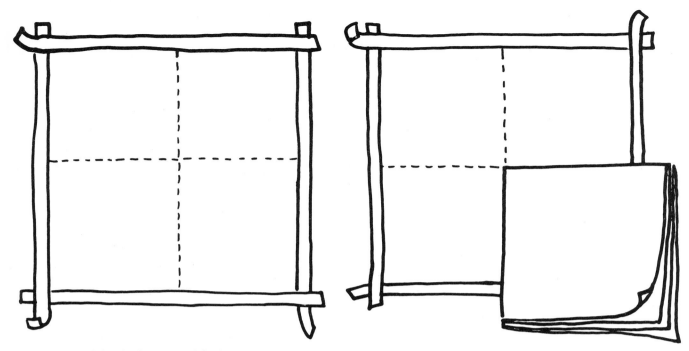

Having folded the material, lay it out and fasten down with masking tape.

Fold the design into four parts and place it in position on one quarter of the fabric.

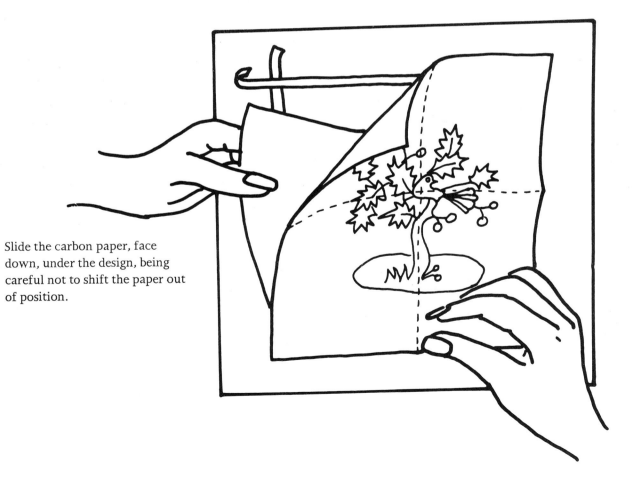

Slide the carbon paper, face down, under the design, being careful not to shift the paper out of position.

Applying the Pattern

MAKING A PRICKING

(1) Break a needle in half and set it into the eraser of an ordinary pencil. You will have to push the needle, blunt end first, into the eraser with a pair of pliers, then you will have a nice short pointed spike sticking out.

(2) Trace the design onto a piece of layout or stout tracing paper, lay this over a pad of felt, or any thick layer of material, placing a sheet of tissue between the two. Now prick holes with your spiked pencil, all around the outlines, holding the pencil vertically – the holes should be fine and close, but as you practice your hand becomes like a machine, working fast and evenly.

(3) First fold both fabric and pricking in four to find the center and hold it in place with weights (as in the carbon method). At a drugstore buy some *powdered* charcoal, and with a rolled and stitched pad of felt, or a blackboard eraser, rub the charcoal through the pricking you have made. Do this quite lightly, rubbing in a circular direction, without using too much charcoal. Lift a corner of the design to check, and if the line is not clear, rub through a little more "pounce" as the charcoal is called. If there is too much already, lift off the pricking and lightly blow off the surplus, leaving a clear line to follow with a brush.

(4) Using a fine watercolor brush (#3 or #4) and a tube of blue watercolor paint, or gouache, paint around all the outlines. You will find the right mixture with practice—too much water, and the line will run, too much paint and it will not flow at all! Always begin at the edge nearest you, covering what you have done with a sheet of tissue paper, so that the pounce will not be smudged by your hand rubbing it. If you do not feel very much like an artist use a ballpoint pen instead. Draw a line with the pen on the corner of the material and test the ink in water first to see if it is fast. On dark material use white watercolor or gouache instead. Finally, bang the design hard with a clean cloth to remove the surplus charcoal – rubbing will smudge it, so flick it until it is clean.

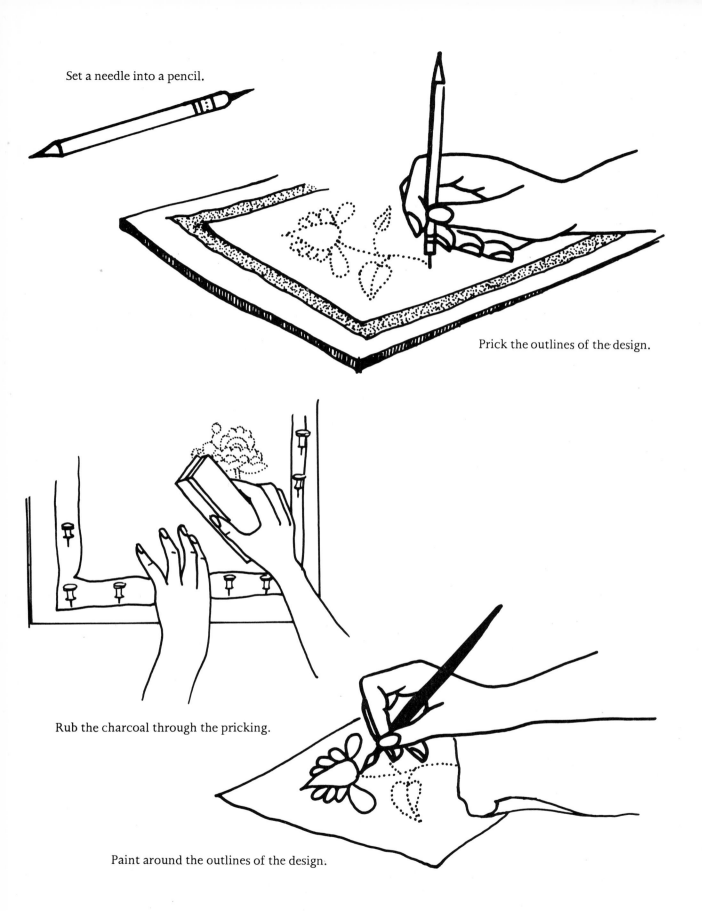

Set a needle into a pencil.

Prick the outlines of the design.

Rub the charcoal through the pricking.

Paint around the outlines of the design.

Applying the Pattern

APPLYING THE DESIGN WITH A TRANSFER PENCIL

This product has arrived on the market lately and is a good short-cut. Using the pink transferring pencil, outline the design on layout or tracing paper, then turn it face downwards onto the material and iron like an ordinary commercial transfer, using a fairly warm iron. The one disadvantage is that it is apt to rub off and it does not provide a very clear fine line. It is therefore most useful for larger bold designs.

Certain fluffy materials, such as wool sweaters, for instance, will not take either paint or carbon well. In this case the only satisfactory method is:

APPLYING THE DESIGN WITH BASTING STITCHES

Buy some batiste, organdie or chiffon, and trace the design through the transparent material, using a hard pencil (of course method 1 and 2 may also be used for this equally well if desired.)

Pin the material with the design to the inside of the sweater. Then baste all around the outlines with small running stitches, using a contrasting color thread. The design will then be transferred onto the right side, and may be embroidered right over the running stitches to cover them.

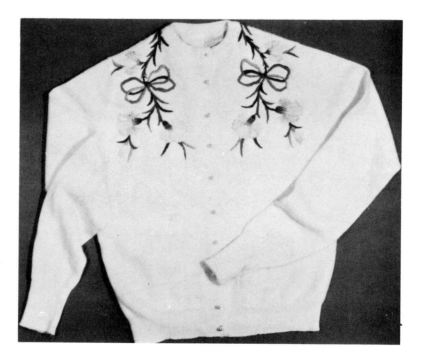

Applying the Pattern

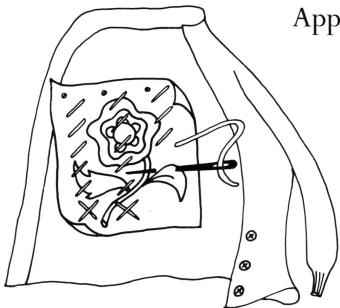

Baste the batiste, with the design on it, to the inside of the sweater.

Baste around the outlines of the design, taking larger stitches on the wool side than on the batiste side.

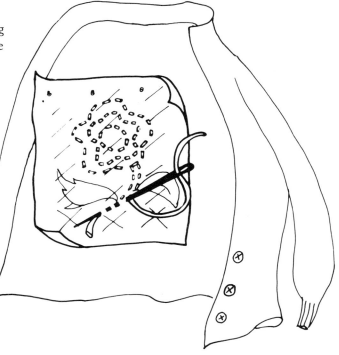

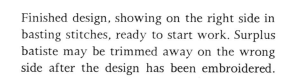

Finished design, showing on the right side in basting stitches, ready to start work. Surplus batiste may be trimmed away on the wrong side after the design has been embroidered.

Choosing a Frame

First of all, is a frame really necessary? If you want to have fun doing a variety of stitches, and your work is to be neat and even, then some sort of frame is a necessity. In fact, it is almost as indispensable as a loom is to a weaver. There are several types to choose from, however. The most useful is probably the ring frame with a floor stand, illustrated here. The ring can be fitted over any section of the work, because the Crewel Work and the linen are tough enough not to be harmed by it, so that a piece of embroidery of any size can be worked. The stand allows you to sit comfortably, working with both hands, one above and one below the frame, necessary for speed and rhythm. When you begin stitching you will find that using your left hand (or right if you are left-handed) feels extraordinary at first, but if you stick to it in the beginning you will be quite used to it after only about an hour of working. After a few days you'll be doing it automatically, and after a week you won't be able to use one hand only!

The other similar variety of frame, equally good, is a ring frame with a table clamp. As shown, it screws on to a table or the arm of a chair, is adjustable as to height and has the advantage of being small enough to carry about. The only disadvantage sometimes is finding a convenient table and not being able to leave the work set up. The floor variety stands in the corner of the room inviting you to sew during the odd ten minutes during the day which are so often wasted. Ring frames *are* made without stands or clamps, and are certainly better than nothing

Standing floor frame, adjustable to height and angle of working.

Choosing a Frame

at all, but they should have an adjustable screw so that the material can be pulled as tight as a drum (essential for all frames) and should be made of wood rather than metal as the latter does not grip well.

The third kind of ring frame is the one which has its own stand, and will rest on a table, or your lap. The advantages of this one are obvious – it is so easy to move about, and is small and compact as well. But the disadvantage of it is that it is inclined to wobble, especially if it is standing on a table – though a heavy book placed on the stand helps to correct this.

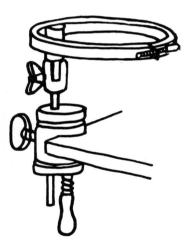

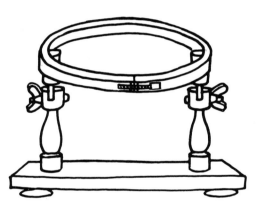

Lap frame, which will stand on a table, with adjustable angle of working.

Table tambour frame, adjustable to height and angle of working.

Simple hoop frame, made of wood, not metal, with a screw adjustment which is best for holding the material really taut.

Choosing a Frame

MOUNTING THE MATERIAL INTO A RING FRAME

First remove the outer hoop of the frame. Lay the material over the inner ring with that part of the design which is to be worked exposed in the center. Tighten the screw of the outer hoop so that it fits down over both the inner ring and the material very snugly. Do not press the hoop all the way down, just push it on so that it fits firmly all round, (as shown in the diagram). The next step is to pull the fabric taut, while simultaneously pressing down on the rim of the frame with your palms, (as shown). Work right round the perimeter in this way until the material is stretched like a drum. Finally press down the outer hoop. It need not be absolutely flat as long as the material is taut.

Wool embroidery on linen is firm enough not to be crushed by having the frame pushed over it when the design has to be moved. The

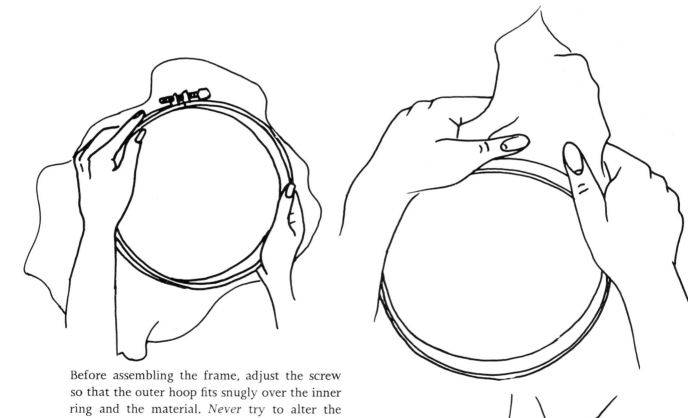

Before assembling the frame, adjust the screw so that the outer hoop fits snugly over the inner ring and the material. *Never* try to alter the screw when the frame is in place.

Pull the material taut; if the upper ring is tight enough the material will not slip back.

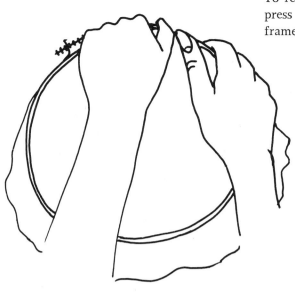

When the material is taut, push the upper ring down. To release the fabric do not unscrew the frame, but press thumbs down firmly into the fabric on the frame, at the same time lifting off the outer ring.

only stitches which might be disturbed are Bullion Knots . . . so it is best to work them last if possible. Delicate fabrics, or those with a satin weave, *may* be marked by the hoop, so place layers of tissue paper over the design before pushing the frame down. Then tear the paper away from the surface of the work, leaving it protecting the fabric round the edge where the hoop would be liable to chafe it.

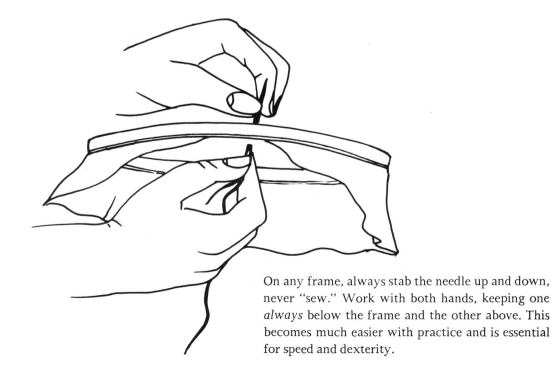

On any frame, always stab the needle up and down, never "sew." Work with both hands, keeping one *always* below the frame and the other above. This becomes much easier with practice and is essential for speed and dexterity.

Stretching and Blocking

When the sampler is finished it may be pressed or blocked. The latter is preferable, for pressing never brings out the very fine creases in heavy material like twill, and pressing is also inclined to pull the article out of shape. If, however, you wish to press an article such as a sweater which cannot be blocked, iron it on the wrong side into three or four thicknesses of towelling, using a damp cloth or steam iron. To block the finished work, first soak the embroidery in cold water, and lay it, dripping wet, on a board or old table which has been first covered with a sheet. If the embroidery is raised, lay it out right side uppermost, if it is flat and a smooth finished result is needed, lay it right side downwards. Then with carpet tacks, nail down the four corners first, measuring the opposite sides to see that they are even and making sure the corners are true right angles. You may have to pull the material out with pliers to make sure it is really taut. Then nail down four more tacks, one in the center of each side, and then eight more in the spaces between. Continue round and round, adding in this way more tacks until they are about a quarter of an inch apart. Allow the fabric to dry. When it is thoroughly dry, take it up, and if it is not being mounted immediately, roll it round a cardboard tube with the embroidery outwards (so that the stitches are not crushed against one another).

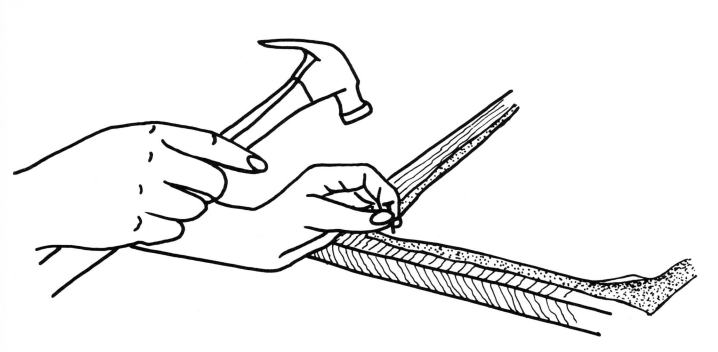

Tack down the design, placing one carpet tack in each corner first.

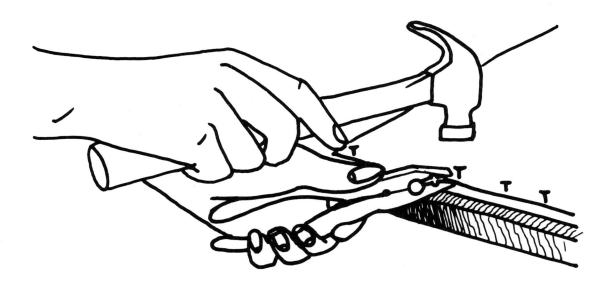

Tack the fabric all around, pulling it out flat with pliers so that it is really taut.

Color

The hardest thing when you are confronted with a glorious array of colors, is to choose and eliminate. The first and most common error in thinking is, "leaves *must* be green, carnations must be pink or white, whoever heard of a purple fish?" etc.! The answer is, of course, if your design is stylized enough, any motif can be any color. Think of a willow pattern plate – blue trees, bridges, houses, people. This is perfect for embroidery, because the simpler the color scheme the more varied can the stitches be without the result becoming too "busy." The easiest way to start is to experiment with several shades of one color (dark, medium or light). Another easy and very effective way is to use all the varieties of one type of color, red, pink, rust, orange, or blue-green, royal blue, blue, purple etc. If you are going to use many colors, pick out the basic ones and let one color predominate, or choose one brilliant color for accent to be used sparingly. Don't be afraid of colors. They never look as bright when they are worked as when they are in the skein. Practice and experience are the only guides here, and the more embroidery you do, the more you will become conscious of color all around you – things like flower arrangements, chintzes, or a turkey carpet will all give you inspiration. Look at your favorite print dress – it is apt to be a color arrangement designed by a professional. If you think that blue and green are not compatible with one another, look at nature and notice how wonderful a green tree looks against the blue sky. The same goes for pinks, reds and oranges as in a sunset. There are no hard and fast rules, yet embroidery with wools is easier than painting – the colors are already there – they don't have to be mixed. It's a good plan to lay out the skeins of wool all over the design before you start, and if necessary move them about – add colors, or take away. This is safer than making a painting to follow – so often the wools cannot be matched to the exact colors in the painting, and the whole effect is lost. A sketch with the dark, medium or light areas roughly put in with either paints or crayon is a great help. This will teach you to look for tone values in colors and then you will know where you want to put the darker more intense colors and vice versa.

Color

Stitches make a great difference here too. The same color used for a closely worked stitch can look twice as dark or bright as the identical color used for an open one.

An 18th century American bed-spread worked entirely in shades of blue. With this simple color scheme contrasts are obtained by working a balance of light powdering stitches and close solid ones.

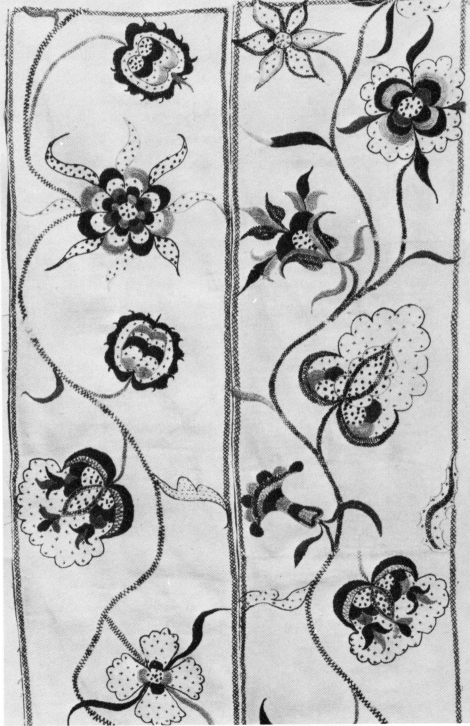

The Stitches

Which comes first?

The hen or the egg?

The design or the stitches?

Many advocates of a free contemporary style suggest starting with a stitch and letting it guide your fancy as you go along. This is a reaction to the mass-produced transfers and partially finished embroideries still unfortunately on sale in many department stores. The lack of imagination and bad taste are enough to quench the spirit of any would-be creative embroiderer. But I feel there is a mid-way course. Once you have done a certain amount of experiment on your sampler, and have become aware of the many sources of inspiration, ideas shouldn't be

This tree was worked with leaves of block shading and French Knot fruits; Burden Stitch to suggest bark on the trunk, and Raised Stem Stitch to give the effect of a wattle fence.

hard to find. If you have had an idea and mapped it out on paper with the limitations of embroidery in mind as you draw, you can decide what sort of stitches you would like for the design. Don't be overwhelmed by the many waiting to be used. No matter which ones you choose when it comes down to the basic elements there are only three ways of using them. Closely for a solid bold effect, widely spaced for lacy open effect, or a happy combination of the two (the most difficult!). A few stitches look best worked open, a few can only be worked solidly, but most are very adaptable and will do either at your will. Simplification is the golden rule, don't try to be too detailed or lose sight of the over-all effect. You are representing an idea, not imitating it. Once you have found the key to translating a form into stitches you can apply it to any design – your eye will become trained to notice and select everything it needs.

The color scheme will influence your choice because when it is mono-chromatic full play can be given to the solid and open effects of the stitches – the same applies to a limited color scheme. This does not mean that a simple pattern might not be extremely effective worked entirely in one stitch and one color. But in these days of enormous variety in printed and woven textiles it is perhaps more interesting to work and look at as an embroidery if there is variation in one or the other. When many colors *and* many stitches are used, though, the result can be over-bearing and fussy unless the design has strong dominating lines or motifs of repeating stitch or color to hold everything together.

Take a plunge and make a start on things you *know* are safe, using the color and stitch you know you want to predominate. Leave the accents for last in small quantities – one brilliant spot of color, or a very few openwork stitches in a closely massed design, or a few wider dominant lines to give character to a uniformly open pattern – and so on. Whatever you do, you will have to experiment and change your ideas as you go along. Experience counts tremendously but even after a great deal of practice it is not always possible to decide which stitch is best the first time. However, don't unpick too much at first! It is much

The Stitches

better to complete a piece of work and look back later, decide what was wrong with it and improve on the next, than to try and have the first design absolutely perfect right away.

Some specific stitches useful for solidly filling a pattern (any one of the following stitches may be used individually for an entire design):

Chain Stitch   Block Shading
Roumanian Stitch   Long and Short
Stem Stitch   Laid Work
Split Stitch

Some specific stitches useful for openwork fillings:

French Knots   Cross Bars (#6, p. 76)
Bullion Knots   Burden Stitch
Herringbone Stitch   Seeding

A handbag, showing an equal balance of open and solid filling stitches. It is worked in blues, greens and pale yellows, using mainly Burden Stitch, Laid Work, Long and Short Stitch, Fishbone Stitch, Padded Satin Stitch and Seeding.

Wools and Needles

Real crewel wool is two-ply wool, firm and not too "stretchy," put out in small hanks with a good variety of colors. There are no rules about whether you should use one, two or more threads for certain stitches. You can vary the number entirely according to the effect you want, light or heavy. This is the advantage of having a fine wool to begin with. Experience and practice will help you decide, and you will find that varying the thickness often in one piece of work helps to create an interesting change of texture, as does combining silk (mercerized cotton will do equally well) with the wool in parts of the design. The beginner always tends to work too tightly. This stretches the wool too much and makes it thin. Experience produces a more even tension, and this difficulty will be overcome – but it can also be avoided at the beginning if short lengths of thread are used, and a needle that is large enough for the thickness of the wool.

Needles should be of medium length but with long eyes. These are available at most stores and come in packets of assorted sizes called either "Crewel" or "Embroidery." Don't make a mistake and buy darners, because though they have large eyes, they are far too long and difficult to handle. When stabbing in and out on a frame your fingers do not hold a long needle near enough to the point and therefore cannot control it properly. Tapestry (blunt) needles are needed too for stitches which are worked mostly on the surface of the material and only occasionally pass through it, such as Weaving Stitch, Spider's Webs, Chain, etc. The higher the number the finer the needle. For instance, the finest crewel needle you would need for wool work would be #8, a good average size is #5, and for very heavy work #3 or #4. In a tapestry needle use #21 or buy a packet of assorted sizes. The needle should always be slightly thicker than the thread, to open up a passage for it to pass through easily – without this, constant passing back and forth will wear out the wool and it will break.

3 – 8

One of a pair of pillows adapted from an 18th century wallpaper in Williamsburg. The colors are terra cotta, brown, dull green and gold.

A design with half an orange in the center, inspired by an 18th century teapot.

Designs for Individual Projects

DESIGNING FROM NATURE

Never forget that you are making an embroidery – something that is to look better in stitchery than any other medium. The main purpose of embroidery is to represent, not to imitate, so keep the design stylized and not photographic. This means observation and elimination; it will show off the stitches to their best advantage, and will also be much more fun to work. Unless the design is completely abstract, do not break the basic laws of nature. For instance, stems and branches never grow downwards from their main stem at an acute angle. Petals radiate from a central axis, and so on. In other words, if natural forms, however stylized, look as though they could grow, the design will have more strength.

TASTE AND IDEAS

A great many books have been published lately concerning the subject of design for embroidery. The authors without exception cry with one voice, "Everyone can draw!" "Design your own work," they say. "Do not rely on hackneyed mass-produced transfers; it's not easy, but practice makes perfect." One author claims that if we had all had as much practice at designing as we have at writing, we could jot down a design as easily as writing "coffee" on our shopping list. This is not necessarily true! With superb optimism, they believe that after reading a few brief instructions one can become a brilliant creative designer. But the truth of the matter is that just as clothes are an expression of our individual taste, and only a few of us make *and* design them ourselves, so the same holds good for embroidery. While originality in design is delightful, there is no harm in drawing inspiration from beautiful historic examples, or from a work of art, and re-creating from them your own embroidery. The artistic expression lies in your free interpretation and your choice of color and stitch. The main idea is being able to differentiate between good and bad, and training the eye to be alert to all the sources of inspiration. Part of the fun of the whole thing is gradually learning what to look for and which design will best suit the limitations of embroidery stitches.

Designs for Individual Projects

DESIGNS WITH CUT-OUT SHAPES

Now you have a sampler finished. You have chosen the material, and you know exactly what you want to make. All you need is the *design*. This may seem a large blank area in your mind. Where to begin? First you need inspiration. The more embroidery you do, the more aware you will become of the possibilities for design, and constant practice at noticing things, and converting them in your mind's eye into an embroidery pattern will open a new world.

You can start slowly – no need to be frightened at having to launch out into the completely unknown to begin with. You have designed your sampler perhaps with very simple lines and geometric shapes. This should have taught you a lesson in space filling, which is that the spaces between the shapes are as important as the shapes themselves. In other words the background material showing through is part of the finished design, and the over-all effect of the *whole* is the important thing. It is a good idea to cut out shapes in paper and arrange them in juxtaposition to one another until you like the arrangement best. Shapes will show off the stitches well if they are simple and stylized, rather than naturalistic or photographic. You can cut out squares, triangles, circles, or indeed any simple forms in colored paper. Arrange them to overlap or fall into groups, and change them freely until the design pleases you. Or you can fold a square of paper in half four or five times. Cut shapes through all the folded thicknesses, and open up the paper again to form a kaleidoscopic pattern.

In all cases keep the design simple, so that the eye is held and led on to the next place easily without being confused by too many motifs competing with one another.

Also, remember the over-all effect, so that the space is filled without leaving large unintentional blank areas or being too overcrowded and cluttered. Study the space the design is to fill, whether it is a circle, an oblong, square, or irregular shape, and arrange the design accordingly

Cut-out designs from folded paper.

This appliquéed quilt shows how simple silhouettes might be filled with suitable repeat stitches most effectively. The stylized shapes mean that full play may be given to the stitches.

Designs for Individual Projects

DOWN-TO-EARTH FACTS TO HELP YOUR DESIGNS

1) *Enlarging Ready-made Designs*

A. BY PHOTOSTATIC REPRODUCTION

If you have a small photograph or drawing of the pattern you want to use you can have it enlarged photostatically. Most towns have a photostatic service, and it is an inexpensive and simple method of making a design larger or smaller. Don't try to give exact all round measurements of the finished size you need. Just measure along one side and the rest will follow naturally. Using clear tracing paper, trace the finished photograph. Both the negative and the positive will be returned to you, so you can choose which is best, but the negative is often clearer.

B. ENLARGING BY SQUARING THE DESIGN

This method is certainly one of the most ancient, but still simple and useful today. It was quaintly but clearly described by Richard Schorleyker in "A Schole House for the Needle" (published in England in 1624). He says, "I would have you knowe, that the use of these squares doth showe how you may contrive to worke any Bird, Beast or Flower into biger or lesser proportions, according as you shall see cause: As thus, if you will enlarge your patterne, devide it into squares, then rule a paper as large as ye list, into what squares you will: Then looke how many holes your patterne doth containe, upon so many holes of your ruled paper drawe your patterne." In case the seventeenth century English is too much for you, the illustration opposite will make things clear!

First square your design, as shown; then take a piece of paper the size the enlargement is to be, and fold it into the same number of squares (this is easier than measuring). Then draw your design to fit within them.

2) *Using Layout Paper to Make Your Own Designs*

As already mentioned in the design for the sampler (page 12) layout paper is ideal to use for making a design. First of all, it is heavy enough to be able to use afterwards for any method of transferring the design to material. Secondly, it is transparent enough to be able to trace through, without constantly erasing, which encourages sureness of line and free style. Therefore if you have a design you want to adapt, trace it first onto a sheet of layout paper, then trace it again and again, using a soft pencil, until it is satisfactory, rather than laboring on one sheet of paper. It's a good idea always to determine the outline of your finished project first, then fold the paper in four so that you have the center lines clearly defined. Then you will never find you have left too much space at the top, or too little on one side, etc. This folding idea is useful when you are making a repeat pattern too. You need only draw one section. Then fold the paper (not more than three times, or it will be too thick) and prick right through all the thicknesses. (See page 16.) This will make the repeat far more accurate than tracing several times.

Introduction to the Stitches

GENERAL NOTES

When beginning a piece of Crewel Embroidery, pick out the shapes which are half covered or which lie under the others, and work these first. For instance, sometimes a stem runs up behind a flower, then the stem should be done first. When a stem runs right up through a leaf, then the *leaf* should be worked first. In this way the shapes which lie on top may be worked so that they really overlap the others, making a clear cut line, with no chance of any material showing through at the joint.

To give your work a crisp and defined look, always exaggerate points; make them sharp by extending the stitches a little beyond the outline indicated. In the same way, when outlining, correct your embroidery to conform to the drawing by either covering or extending beyond the previous stitches.

A contemporary version of the Tree of Life design. The back of the chair was worked as the chair stands in the room where this would show.

Bedspread worked in squares and joined together with piping.

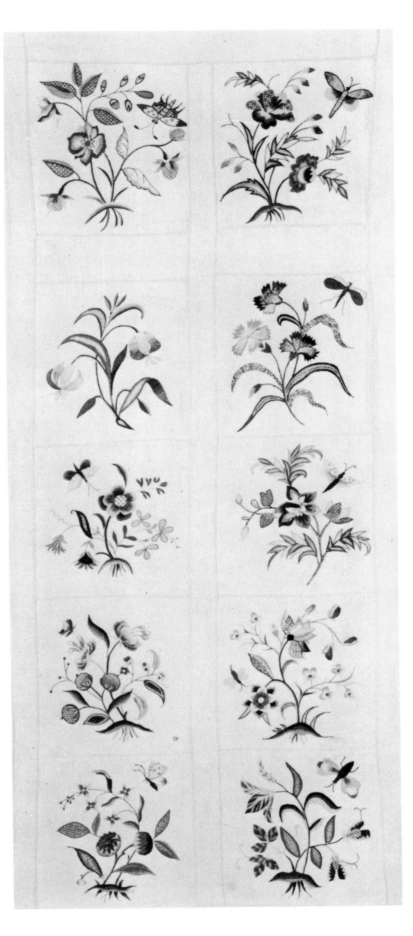

A bell-pull worked with light open stitches in the leaves and a solid stem to give continuity to the design.

Introduction to the Stitches

Many stitches can be worked either in the hand or on a frame, which-ever is preferred. Those stitches for which a frame is really essential are marked with an asterisk.

When the work is stretched tightly on a frame, the needle must always be stabbed straight up and down, never sewn. In order to make the diagrams of certain stitches clearer, the needle sometimes had to be shown *sewing* through the material. When this is the case, simply stab up and down at the letters indicated.

When working on a frame, be sure to hold the needle near the point, to control it better.

Put it in and bring it up really vertically, never on a slant. Then your stitches will be more accurate.

When there seems nowhere to end off your thread – every surround-ing line is covered – tuck the two back stitches *under* the nearest worked stitches. Pull the thread quite tight and it will never show.

Most of the stitches are equally good worked either with single or double thread. A few, however, really look best when worked with two or more threads. They are the following :

Coral, Rope, Braid, French and Bullion Knots, Turkey Work, Couch-ing, Raised Stem Stitch, Knotted Pearl Stitch, Weaving Stitch, Chain Stitch.

Generally speaking, also, Satin Stitch is easier to make when it is worked with single thread. These rules only hold true for a normal effect, however, and for a larger or smaller scale any desired number of threads may be used.

Threading the Needle

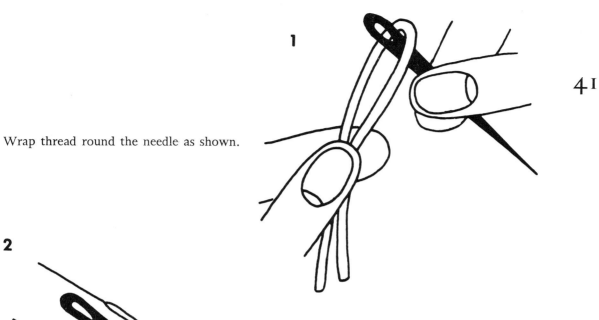

1

Wrap thread round the needle as shown.

2

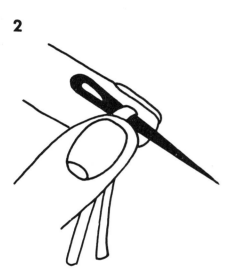

Hold thread tightly, close round needle; pull needle away.

3

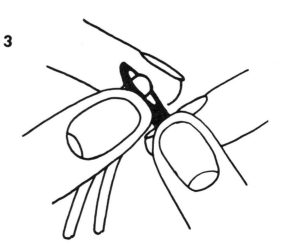

Squeeze thread *tightly* between finger and thumb, so that thread is almost buried. Press eye of needle flat down on to it. (Push the needle down on to the thread, rather than attempting to push the thread through the needle.) Pull through when amount of thread shown in diagram has appeared.

Starting and Ending Off

1

Put a knot in the thread and start on the wrong side of the material. As crewel work should always be backed, the wrong side is not of such tremendous importance, though care should be taken to keep the stitches flat, and not to jump too far from place to place without taking a small stitch in between (to prevent leaving a long loose thread on the wrong side).

2

End off with 2 small back stitches on an outline or inside the shape of a design which will later be covered. (The stitches in the diagram are enlarged to show clearly – they should be very small.) Come up at A and pull through at B, then bring thread to front of work near by and cut off.

Line Stitches

Like their name, these stitches make continuous lines and are useful
worked either singly or in close rows to completely fill an area.

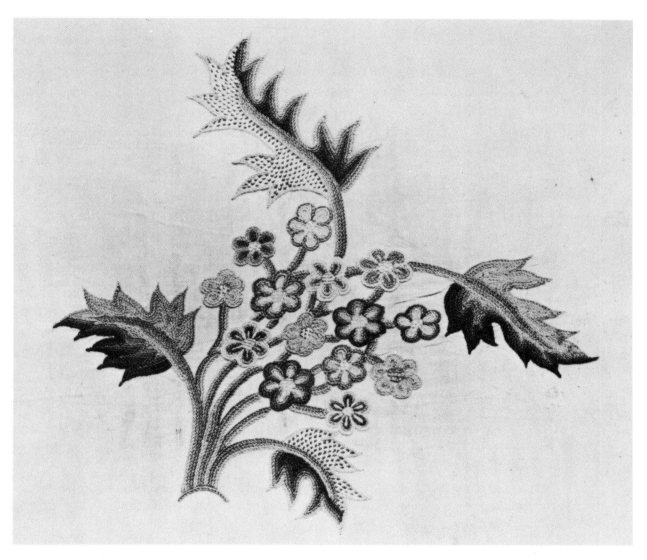

Chain Stitch

44

Chain Stitch may be used as a solid filling, working row upon row closely side by side. Do not pack the stitches *too* closely, however, or the effect will be lost. The filling is equally effective if the lines are shaded, or worked all in one color with contrasting outline. (The stitches should all begin at the same end and run in the same direction to make a smooth effect). When extra lines have to be added to broaden the shape in one place, add them on the inside, allowing a continuous line to run along the edges. In this way the joining lines will not be obvious, especially if the first stitch of the joining line is tucked *underneath* the longer line.

Chain Stitch may also be used as an outline where a fairly broad dominant edge is needed.

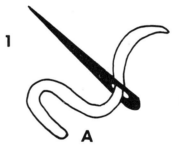

Bring needle up at A.

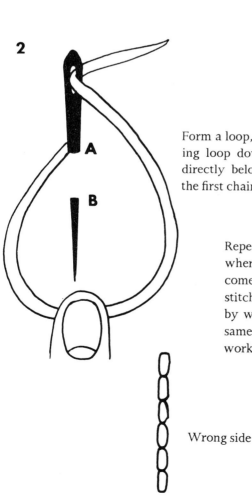

Form a loop, and put the needle in at A again, holding loop down with finger. Then come up at B, directly below A. Draw gently through, forming the first chain stitch.

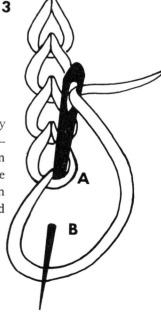

Repeat # 2, always inserting needle exactly where the thread came out, *inside* the last loop – come up directly below, and draw through so chain stitches lie flat on material. When filling a shape by working rows of Chain Stitch, always work in same direction, beginning each new row at top and working down.

Wrong side

Stem Stitch

An excellent outline stitch, Stem Stitch may also be used as a solid filling. In this case, like Chain Stitch, the lines should all be worked in the same direction for smoothness. The thread may be held either to the right or left of the needle, but once a line or a block of stitches is begun it should be held always to the same side. When working outlining, hold the thread away from the shape and towards the outside of curves. This will make the outline "roll" outwards instead of falling inwards and becoming "spikey".

When working stems and branches, work the main stem right through first, from top to bottom. Then, starting at the tips of the subsidiary stems, work them down to join the main stem, continuing the line alongside for several stitches to make a smooth join. Shorten the stitches slightly when working curves.

1

Needle comes up at A, goes in at B, and up again at C, exactly half way between A and B. Draw through, holding the thread to the left of the needle.

2

Needle goes in at D, up again at B, (in the same hole made by the thread going in previously at B). Draw through, still holding thread to left of needle.

3

Continue by repeating #2. The thread may be held either to the right or the left of the needle, but should remain on the same side once the work is started.

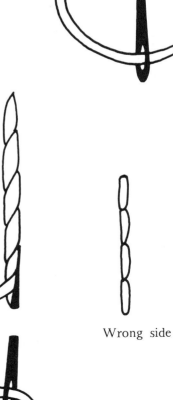

Wrong side

*Split Stitch

Like Stem and Chain Stitch, Split Stitch may be worked in close lines all in one direction. It is especially effective worked in one color when the only interest lies in the direction of line. It may be used as an outline stitch but it is more useful as an underlying padding on an edge which will later be covered with other stitching.

1

Needle comes up at A, goes down at B.

2

Needle comes up at C piercing through center of stitch from below, splitting it exactly in the middle.

Needle goes down at D, a little ahead of B—(the distance from C to D is the same as the length of the first stitch; from A to B.) Repeat in this way, forming a smooth line of stitching slightly shortening the stitches when going around curves.

3

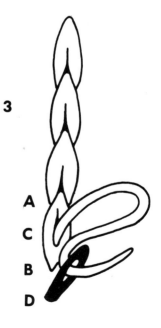

Buttonhole Stitch

This is one of the most versatile of stitches. It may be worked in solid rows, or radiating from one central point to form a circle, in scallops, or with the spokes outwards as an outline around a shape. (This was frequently used in Jacobean embroidery to soften the edge of large leaves). Always space the stitches just far enough apart to allow the loops at the edge to lie smoothly. Like Chain Stitch, Buttonhole Stitch is the basis for many other stitches, notably Coral Stitch.

1

Needle comes up at A, goes in at B, and up at C directly below B, and level with A. Thread is held under needle as in diagram. Draw through downwards.

2

Next stitch repeats #1 at an even distance apart. Stitching may be spaced as shown, or worked closely as in #3.

3

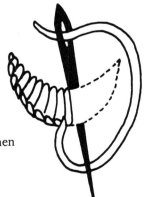

Diagram shows angle of needle when working curved shapes.

Coral Stitch

The knots may be spaced closely or far apart, but should always be at right angles to the line. When several rows are worked close together the stitches should be fitted into the spaces between the knots on the previous lines. The effect of the stitching when it is solid is almost like rows of fat French Knots. To make it effective it is best to use double thread.

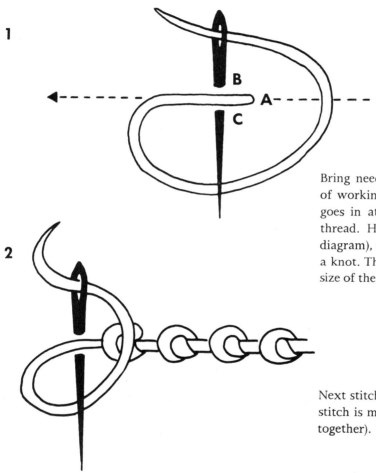

1

2

Bring needle up at A, lay thread flat in direction of working (indicated by dotted line.) Needle then goes in at B, and up at C at right angles to the thread. Holding the thread under needle (as in diagram), draw through and pull gently up to form a knot. The space between B and C determines the size of the knot.

Next stitch repeats #1 a little distance away. (The stitch is more effective if the knots are fairly close together).

 Wrong side

Braid Stitch

Braid stitch is strictly an outline stitch, as it would be difficult to work rows close together without the needle interfering with the previous row. Single thread may be used, but double thread will show the stitch to its best advantage.

1

Make a small Chain Stitch. Come up at A, and go down again at A, holding the loop open—come up inside this loop at B and draw flat.

Anchor this Chain Stitch by going down outside the loop at C.

2

3

Using a blunt needle, come up at D and slide through the Chain Stitch (not through the material) from right to left (as shown).

4

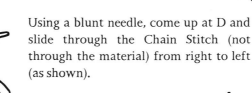

Then go down at D through the material.

5

Next come up at E, just below D. Slide the needle from right to left under the anchoring stitch B-C, as well as the last chain just completed (diagram #4). Do not go through material.

6

Go down through the material at E.

7

Come up at F and going back two stitches, slide the needle from right to left under both of them (as shown).

Continue in this way, sliding the needle from right to left under the two previous stitches together. Go down into the material where the thread came up, and come up again below ready to repeat.

8

9

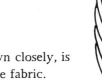

The finished effect, drawn closely, is like a braid on top of the fabric.

Rope Stitch (narrow)

This stitch may be used as an outline, or as a solid filling, working the rows close together, all in the same direction. It is difficult to make this stitch smooth without practicing a little first, but it helps if the stitches are fairly long. Use double thread.

1

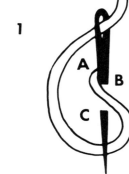

Come up at A and go down at B, immediately below A. Form a loop and come up at C, directly below B and inside the loop; draw flat. This stitch is like Chain, except that the thread is crossed in front of the needle before looping under it, and exactly like Rope Stitch – Broad, except that the needle is almost straight, instead of slanting.

2

Go down at D, pushing the needle very close up into the waist formed by the twisted chain. Looping the thread under the needle, come up at E on a straight line below A; draw flat.

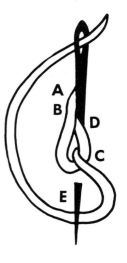

3

Repeat #2, and continue along the line. A smooth effect will be gained only if the needle is pushed very close, almost under the stitches (at arrow). The stitch must also be pulled down toward you to tighten it, or the loop will not lie flat.

4

Finished effect

Rope Stitch (broad)

This stitch is really exactly like Narrow Rope Stitch, except that the position of the needle is different. Used for a stem, Broad Rope appears rather like a Slanting Satin Stitch band, flat on one side and raised on the other. It may be worked as a solid filling, or a line of rope may be worked sometimes broad and sometimes narrow in one continuous line.

1

Come up at A and go down at B, tucking the needle just under A (as shown). Bring the needle out at C, twisting the thread first over and across the needle, then under it (as shown). Draw flat, pulling the thread taut in the direction of the arrow. The slant of the needle from B to C is about 45°.

2

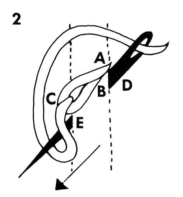

Go in at D, and come up at E, parallel with, and just touching A-C. Twist the thread over and then under the needle as before, and draw it flat, taking care not to let the loop rise up before the thread is tight. It is very easy to lose the slant and flatten out when working this stitch. To maintain the 45° angle keep the needle at D very close and touching A. Come up at E a *slight* distance below C; and again draw flat in the direction of the arrow to keep the loops lying smooth.

3

If the angle is maintained, a smooth Satin Stitch effect will result (as in diagram).

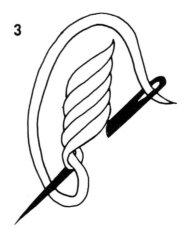

*Couching

Couching may be worked as a plain outline, having the couching threads the same color as those underneath. Either one or two threads may be used in the needle and any number of threads may be couched down. Or two contrasting colors may be used, and the top stitches worked to form patterns. Couching may be used as a solid filling, working the threads back and forth or round in circles, or following the shape of the motif being filled. It may also be used as an open filling, called Random Couching, and is worked in any direction until the ground is evenly but lightly filled.

52

1

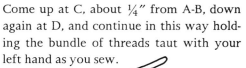

Lay a bundle of threads (in this case 3) along the line, and with one thread in the needle come up at A, in at B. (B is almost in the same hole as A.)

2

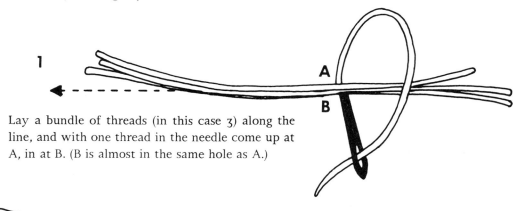

Come up at C, about ¼″ from A-B, down again at D, and continue in this way holding the bundle of threads taut with your left hand as you sew.

When the line is completed, thread the 3 threads into a large-eyed needle, plunge them through the material exactly in the hole made by the last couching stitch and cut them off short (about ¼″) on reverse side.

3

4

Patterns may be made with the couching stitches (brick stitch shown). Always bring needle up on the outside, and go down close to the line already worked, so that no material shows between lines of couching. At the corners work couching stitch at the angle shown to make a sharp corner without having to plunge threads at the end of each line.

Rosette Chain Stitch

It is best worked fairly small and closely, too large a stitch can easily become caught and pull when in use. It is most effective as a single line or edging.

1

Working on a line from right to left, using a blunt needle, come up at A, go down at B, a little to the left and below A, and come up at C, slightly to the right and below B. Hold the thread across in front of the needle, then twist it under the needle, as shown. Pull through, keeping the stitch lying flat on the material.

2

Now slide needle under the stitch at A, as shown. Do not pass through the material.

Then repeat #1, a little distance away from the stitch just made, but level with it.

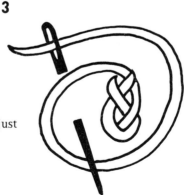

3

Repeat along the line. The effect of this stitch can be varied by placing the "rosettes" near one another or further apart.

4

Zig-zag Chain Stitch

Like Interlaced Running, this stitch needs space to show it to its best advantage.

This stitch is exactly like Chain Stitch, except that every stitch is worked at an angle to the previous one, as shown. The angle may be increased or decreased according to the effect required.

Band Stitches

These stitches might also be called broad line stitches for they make bands which may be worked singly or in lines close together to fill an area.

Roumanian Stitch

Roumanian Stitch is really a straight Satin Stitch tied down with a smaller slanting stitch in the center. If the small stitch maintains its slant well, the stitches will fit closely together with no separation between them, keeping the effect smooth. However, this small stitch may be worked on a greater slant if the area to be filled is wide. When several bands are worked side by side the stitches should just overlap one another at the edge. If each row fits into the *exact* holes of the previous one, the stitches are apt to pull away a little and leave material showing in between.

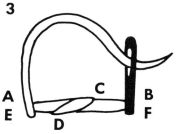

Come up at A, down at B; pull flat.

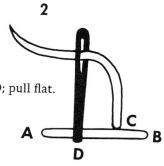

Come up at C and go over and down at D; pull flat.

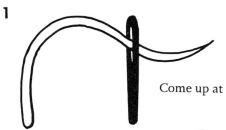

Next, come up at E, below but touching A, go down at F, below but touching B; leave a loop.

Then come up at G, close to and immediately below C, inside the loop; draw tight.

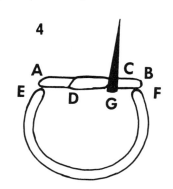

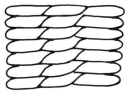

Go down over thread at H, directly below D, exactly as in #2, and continue; repeating #3, 4, 5. Keep center row of stitches G-H even, (as shown in finished effect).

Finished effect

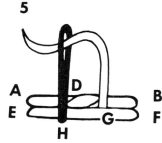

Cretan Stitch

This stitch may be worked very close and slanting, as shown, or flatter and with spaces between the stitches. In this way two completely different effects may be obtained, just as in Fishbone Stitch.

1

2

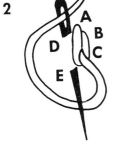

Come up at A. Go down at B a fraction below and to the right of A. Form a loop and come up at C inside the loop.

Go down at D, a fraction to the left and below A. Form a loop and come up at E, inside the loop. E is a little to the left and below C.

3

Repeat #1, going down at F and up at G, inside the loop as shown. F and G are a fraction to the right and below the previous stitches.

4

Repeat #2. Needle goes down and comes up a fraction to the left and below other stitches, coming up inside the loop each time.

5

Continue in this way so that a plait is formed down the center of the shape. Keep the stitches very close together on the edge to maintain the slant, and the center stitches on an even line below one another, as shown.

6  Finished effect

Van Dyke Stitch

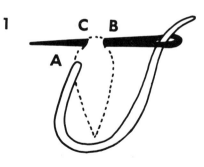

Using a blunt needle, come up at A and take a small stitch from B to C at top of shape to be worked (as shown).

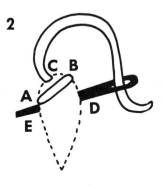

Go down at D and up at E, a needle's width below A on the outline.

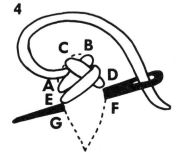

Slide needle from right to left under the Cross Stitch formed by A-B, and C-D. Do not go through the material.

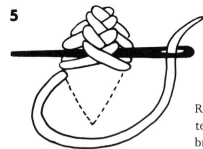

Go down at F on the outline, a needle's width below D. Come up at G below E on the outline.

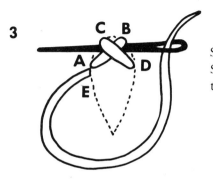

Repeat #3 and #4 until shape is filled. If the tension is even (do not pull too tightly), a raised braid will be formed smoothly down the center.

Knotted Pearl Stitch

The Buttonhole Stitches should not be pulled too tight, and should always be drawn up into the center of the band, to make a row of raised knots down the middle of the stitch. Do not attempt to work too wide a band with it.

Come up at A, go down at B, and up again at C. A-B-C are all on a straight line (as shown).

1

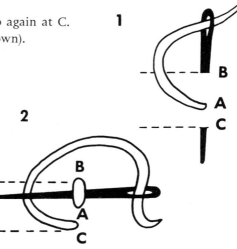

Using a blunt needle, slide under stitch B-A from right to left without going through material. Holding loop under the needle (as shown), pull flat. This forms one Buttonhole Stitch on bar B-A.

2

3

Now work a second Buttonhole Stitch by going under the bar B-A again, exactly as in #2.

4

Go down through the material at D, come up at E. D and E are level with B and C (as shown).

5

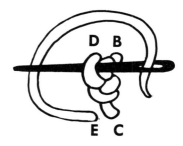

Now repeat procedure of #2 again . . . this time the Buttonhole Stitches are worked into the bar at D (as shown). Be very careful to pick up only the bar at D and not the other stitches.

6

Finished effect. To complete row, go down outside last Buttonhole loop to anchor it.

Herringbone Stitch

This stitch is the simple foundation for many variations. It may be worked as broad or narrow as desired and may require a little practice at first to keep it regularly spaced and even.

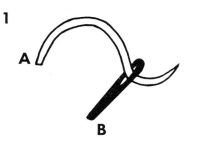

Come up at A, go down at B, diagonally below A.

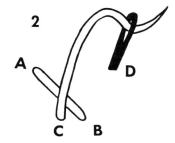

Come up at C, a little to the left, and level with B, and go down at D, level with A, making a diagonal stitch in the other direction.

Come up at E, a little to the left and level with D, go down at F. E to F is another diagonal stitch parallel with A-B. Repeat from #2 again.

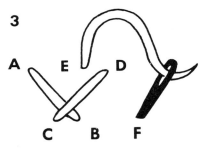

Continue repeating #2 and #3, spacing the stitches evenly so that the diagonals are parallel.

Close Herringbone Stitch

This stitch is smoothest if kept slanting. Space the stitches a little apart when the needle goes down, and keep them close together (almost touching) when the needle comes up on the edge. This will help maintain the slant, and make a sharp V in the center. It is attractive when used on small leaves.

1

Come up at A, go down at B, diagonally below A.

2

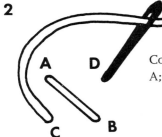

Come up at C, go down at D (C is directly below A; D is directly above B).

Come up at E, close to A, go down at F, close to B.

3

4

Come up at G, close to C, go down at H close to D.

Continue in this way along the line, forming a solid band of stitching.

5

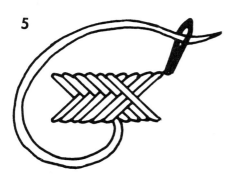

6

To work a shape as above, start exactly on point A and work in direction of B, coming up and down on outline so that stitches automatically fill the shape.

Fishbone Stitch

The first stitch (A to B) should be at least ¼″ long to start the stitch off on a good slant. To maintain this slant, bring the needle up and go down on the edge, almost in the same holes as the previous stitches, and keep the center stitch (B to E) a good length. The stitch looks best if a smooth edge is made which does not need outlining afterwards. Like Cretan, Fishbone may also be worked with spaces between the stitches for an open effect.

1

Come up at A in the center of point. Go down at B directly below it—(draw line down center as guide line.) Come up at C to left and slightly below A, but touching it, on outline of shape.

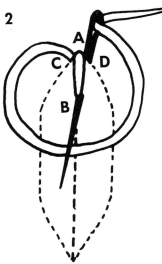

2

Go in at D to right and slightly below A, but touching it. Come up at B, and form a loop by holding thread under needle.

3

Draw through and insert needle at E a short space directly below B, come up at F—again to the left and slightly below C, but touching it.

4

Now repeat #2 again; come up at F, go in at G (touching previous threads). Come up at E with thread under the needle. Anchor it down as in #3, and continue in this way.

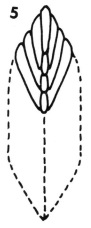

5

Finished effect.

Raised Stem Stitch [*]

Though it is shown here as a banding stitch, Raised Stem may be used to fill whole areas. In this case the long basic stitches should be tacked down invisibly here and there, afterwards. The stitch may be shaded, working in vertical bands, or stripes of contrasting colors. When used to fill an uneven area it usually needs an outline of Stem Stitch.

1

First work a series of parallel stitches (just under ¼″ apart, as shown in diagram). To work a wider area than the one shown, lay these lines across the whole width of the shape.

A   B

2

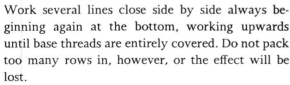

Using a blunt (tapestry) needle, come up at A, and holding thread to left of needle slide under first thread from B to C. Do not go through material.

3

Repeat #2, sliding needle under thread from D to E, and work up to top of thread in this way.

Work several lines close side by side always beginning again at the bottom, working upwards until base threads are entirely covered. Do not pack too many rows in, however, or the effect will be lost.

4

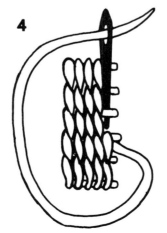

*Raised Chain Stitch

See notes on Raised Stem Stitch.

64   **1**

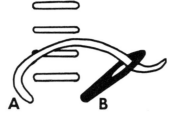

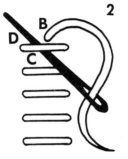

First work a series of parallel stitches (just under ¼″ apart) as shown in diagram. (As for Raised Stem Stitch.)

2

Then bring thread up at B and slide under thread from C to D (do not go through material). This stitch is best worked with a blunt needle. Draw through and hold thread upwards keeping it rather taut.

3

Next slide needle downwards under same thread, but to the right of first stitch, from E to F, draw through, holding thread under needle; do not pull too tightly so the appearance of the stitch is as in #4.

4

Continue stitch by repeating #2 and #3. Several rows may be worked side by side to fill a space (as in Raised Stem Stitch) instead of single row shown. In this case end off row at base and start again at the top, ready to work downwards.

Raised Buttonhole Stitch[*]

See notes on Raised Stem Stitch.

1

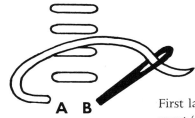

First lay a series of parallel stitches just under ¼″ apart (as shown in diagram).

2

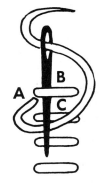

Using a blunt needle, come up at A, form a loop with the thread, and without going through the material, slide under the first bar from B to C (as shown). Draw down towards you until the thread is snug. This forms a Buttonhole Stitch on the horizontal bar.

3

Repeat #2, sliding the needle under the thread from D to E, and work to the bottom of the bars in this way. When you have reached the bottom of each line, anchor the final stitch by going down through the material over the buttonhole loop at F (as in diagram #4).

4

Work several lines close side by side, always beginning at the top, working downwards, until the bars are entirely covered. Do not pack too many rows in or the effect will be lost.

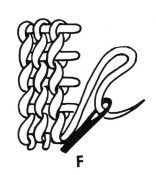

Filling Stitches

As indicated by their name, these stitches may be used to fill areas with solid or lacy effects as needed.

Slanting Satin Stitch*

This stitch needs practice in order to make it neat and even. The slant helps to make it smoother, and the Split Stitch padding makes it easier to keep the edge clean; both essential to the effect. It should never be used for large areas, because the threads could easily be pulled and disarranged when the embroidery is in use. On very small leaves it is easier to start at the tip and work downwards. To maintain the slant, come up close at the upper edge and go down with a slight space between the stitches on the lower edge. This tends to exaggerate the slant of each stitch but prevents them from flattening out.

1

First outline shape with Split Stitch.

2

Starting in the center (to be certain of the exact angle), work slanting stitches close together across the shape, coming up and going down outside the Split Stitch. (Split Stitch forms a padding on the outline, giving a firm edge.)

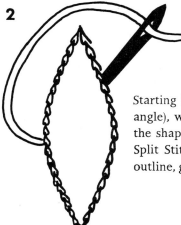

3

Work up to tip, then start at center again and finish working shape to the bottom. Stitches should lie evenly side by side, not crowded, but no material showing between. Do not pull too tightly.

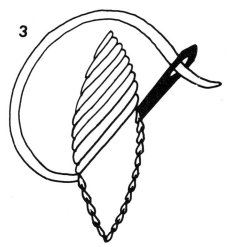

*Satin Stitch — Tied with Back Stitch

This stitch may be used to fill a wider area, for unlike Slanting Satin Stitch, it has a row of stitching to hold it in the center. More than one row of Back Stitch may be worked if the area needs it. Do not pull the Back Stitch too tight for it will spoil the evenness of the Satin Stitch underneath it.

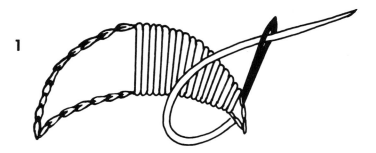

Having outlined shape with Split Stitch, Satin Stitch over it, starting in center to guide stitches at the correct angle. Keep stitches fairly upright at outside points (as shown). It is easier to work longer stitches instead of very short ones.

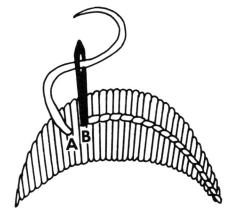

As stitches would be too long to leave untied, work a row of Back Stitch through the center of the shape, using the upper edge as a guide line. Needle comes up at A, and down at B, right into the hole made by the last stitch.

Padded Satin Stitch *

The top row of Padded Satin Stitch may be worked straight instead of slanting, but this is much harder to make even, especially when the stitches are small at the point of a leaf. It is therefore best to practice it on a slant first.

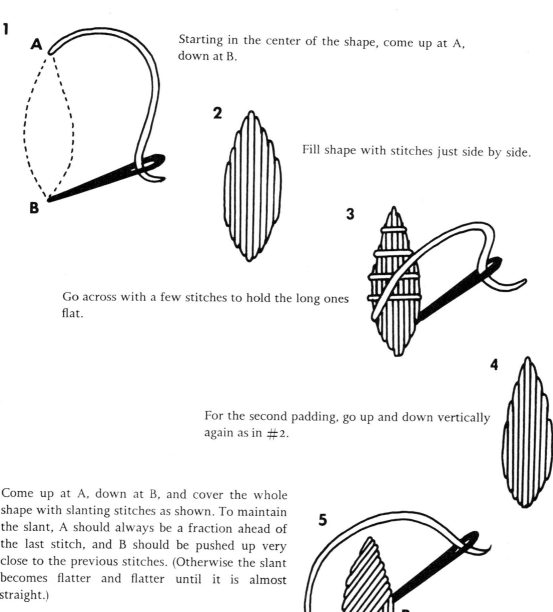

Starting in the center of the shape, come up at A, down at B.

Fill shape with stitches just side by side.

Go across with a few stitches to hold the long ones flat.

For the second padding, go up and down vertically again as in #2.

Come up at A, down at B, and cover the whole shape with slanting stitches as shown. To maintain the slant, A should always be a fraction ahead of the last stitch, and B should be pushed up very close to the previous stitches. (Otherwise the slant becomes flatter and flatter until it is almost straight.)

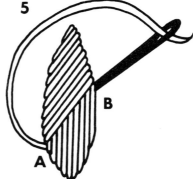

* Block Shading

Like Roumanian Stitch, bands of Block Shading should fit closely together, slightly overlapping the previous row, to prevent any material showing between them. Never outline Block Shading afterwards, the edge will be smooth and raised because of the Split Stitch padding.

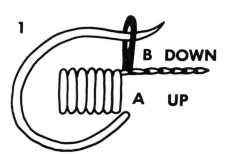

First outline shape to be worked with Split Stitch. Then work a row of Satin Stitches, bringing needle up at A, down at B, over Split Stitch. (This makes a firm, even edge.) Keep all the stitches close and even, side by side.

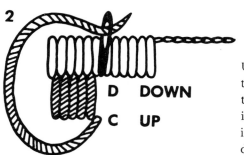

Using the next shade, work a second row, repeating the first exactly. Come up at C, down at D, just between the stitches of the previous row. Block shading consists of even bands of Satin Stitches, changing color with each row, but showing a clear division between each band.

3

To work round a curve, place the stitches slightly wider apart on the edge, closer in the center to fan them, leaving no visible space between them, however. Occasionally slip in a shorter wedge stitch to help fan them (as shown in the diagram by the arrow).

Long and Short Stitch – Tapestry Shading *

Whole designs, including the background, may be worked in Tapestry Shading. The effect will be like its name; the vertical shading of tapestry. This is a good stitch to practice before trying Long and Short – Soft Shading, since you can experiment with the size of the stitch and correct blending of the colors without having to bother about changing direction. Use double thread for practicing so that the stitches are clear. Though the colors should blend, it is better to have a clearly defined difference between them to show the stitch to its best advantage. In spite of the difference in length of the stitches, the rows should be as regular and definite as those in Block Shading. An outline afterwards will spoil the effect of the raised edge obtained by the Split Stitch padding.

First work a row of Split Stitch along the outline. This stitch will be covered by Long and Short, but it is valuable as a firm padding and enables you to make a knife-sharp edge with the Long and Short. Come up at A and go down at B just *over* Split Stitch. Work a row of Long and Short Stitches side by side, as in diagram. (The short stitch is ¾ of the length of the long one.) Keep each long stitch alike and all the short stitches the same length.

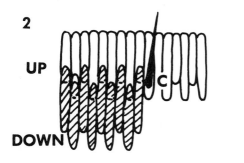

Next row. In another shade, *split up* through the first long and short stitches ¼ of the way back, at C. Go down into the material at D. These stitches are all of equal length, but are staggered in brick fashion to fit up into the long and short previous row. The dotted line on diagram shows how much of each previous stitch lies under the succeeding row.

In a third color, work a third line of stitches the same way (repeating #2), always coming up ¼ of the way back through the stitch. Be sure each row is long enough. Remember ¼ of the stitch will be obscured when the succeeding row is worked into it, and allow for this. Any number of rows may be worked in this way, using any number of colors, or only one. The best effect is obtained, however, if the rows are shaded gradually from dark to light, or light to dark, as in diagram.

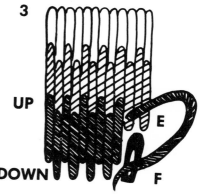

* Long and Short (continued)

Long and Short – Soft Shading repeats the principle of Tapestry Shading exactly. Instead of running straight up and down, however, the stitches follow direction lines as indicated in the diagrams.

First draw guide lines in pencil on the material (as shown by dotted lines). Then outline the shape with Split Stitch, both the inner ring and outer petals. Next work the first row of Long and Short, coming up at A and going down *over* the Split Stitch at B, starting in the center (or highest point) of each petal. It is easier to work downwards from the center on either side, since the angle of the stitch is straight to begin with, then gradually fans very slightly on each side. To achieve this, the stitches may be placed slightly wider apart on the outside edge and closer in the center, exactly like a fan. If this is not sufficient, a greater slant may be obtained by taking an extra short stitch over the upper edge occasionally (as indicated by the arrow in the diagram). This "wedge stitch" will not show, providing the next stitch is taken extremely close to it. On the shape illustrated, few wedge stitches are necessary since all the stitches gravitate to the center of the flower like the spokes of a wheel.

1

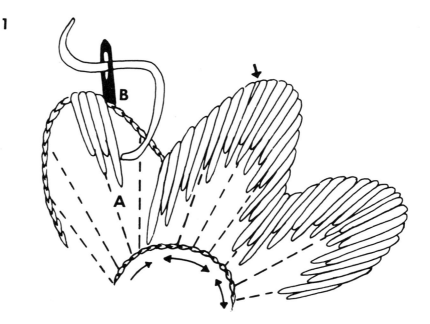

2

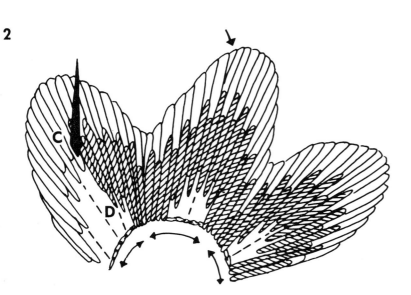

Work a second row of stitches in the next shade lighter or darker, coming up at C and down at D. Here again the stitches fan slightly as in the first row. They should not change direction abruptly, but should flow into one another smoothly. As in Tapestry Shading, be sure to split far enough back into the previous row and make the stitches long enough for the third row to split into them.

In the shape illustrated this second row of stitches comes right over the outline at the lowest point of the petals (as shown).

With the third color, fill the remaining spaces in the center of each petal only. Come up at E and go down at F. Bring the stitches evenly down *over* the Split Stitch, making a smooth outline as at the beginning. On the third row it is impossible to fit each stitch *exactly* back through the previous stitch; every now and again miss one (as in the diagram). This is because there is less space in the center of the curve than on the outside. Still make the stitches look regular, keeping a long and short effect.

3

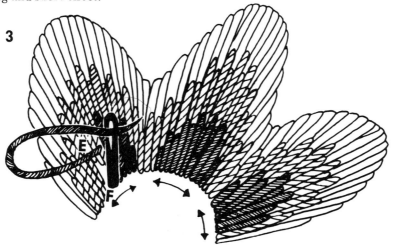

Turkey Work

If the loops get in the way while working, pin them down to the material. Do not be afraid to cut the loops down in the end, the result is neater if the effect is like a piece of thick velvet. It is always easier to work the stitch in rows horizontally regardless of what shape is being filled.

1

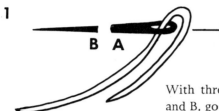

Go down at A, come up at B. Do not knot the thread, but leave about 1" hanging on top, (as shown in diagram #2). Arrow indicates direction of working.

With thread *below* the needle, on a line with A and B, go down at C, and come up in same hole as A. Draw this stitch tight, holding on to the loose end of thread, (so that it does not pull right through the material).

2

3

With the thread *above* the needle, go down at D, come up in the same hole as C. *Do not* draw tight, but leave a loop, (as shown). In this stitch, the needle should always be horizontal. (In order to show the stitch clearly in the diagram, it has been drawn on a slant.)

With the thread once more *below* the needle, go in at E, and up in the same hole as D; pull tight.

4

5

Continue along the line, coming up each time into the hole made by the previous stitch. The thread is alternately above the needle, leaving a loop, and below the needle drawing it tight.

Finished effect of single line. Work this stitch in lines one after the other. To achieve a thick velvety effect at the end, take small stitches and work the lines very close together. (This working diagram is much enlarged.)

6

7

Having filled the shape, cut all the loops along dotted line (as shown in diagram). Do not cut each line individually; trim the whole shape to the desired length, (a full 1/8" long).

8

Finished effect

LAID WORK TIED WITH CROSS BARS—
LAID WORK TIED DIAGONALLY–SHADED LAID WORK

This is a most useful stitch for covering large areas, either in one color or several. It must be tied down afterwards, or the long threads would catch when the embroidery was in use. This tying down may be done in many ways as shown on the subsequent pages, either with criss-crossing lines, parallel lines tied down with a small tacking stitch, with Split Stitch, Coral, or practically any other line stitch. The first three are the most usual because they do not disturb the Laid Stitches underneath, but Laid Work is very versatile, and even open fillings such as Burden Stitch may be used to cover it. It is usually best to lay the lines across the longest direction of the shape but remember the tie-down stitches will predominate, and as these will run in the opposite direction to the first layer, consider this before starting. Always start laying the basic threads across the center or broadest part of the design to set the direction. Small awkward corners are then easier to fill in later. A strong outline afterwards is essential.

TIED WITH CROSS BARS

Needle comes up at A, goes in at B right across widest point of shape, to establish desired direction. All subsequent stitches are parallel to this line.

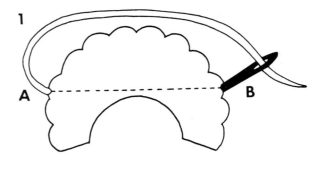

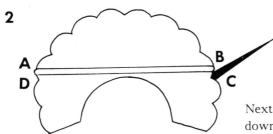

Next stitch comes up at C, close to B, and goes down again at D, close to A.

3

Continue working in this way, coming up close beneath previous stitch, on the same side as where you went down. (Stitches should lie evenly side by side with no material showing between them.) When lower half is completed go back to center and work upper half in same way.

4

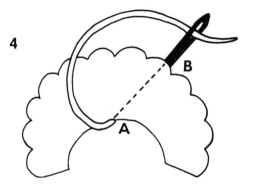

Starting in broadest part of shape come up at A, down at B, laying a long thread diagonally across shape (angle is indicated by dotted line). This should cut across Laid Work threads at about 45°.

5

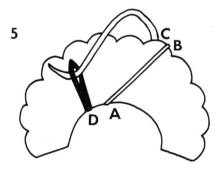

Come up at C, about ¼″ away from B, and go in at D, making a line parallel to A and B. Cover the whole shape in this way, and then work lines in the other direction to make perfect diamonds as shown in #6.

6

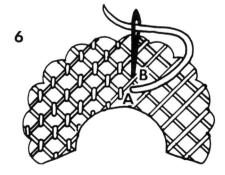

These threads are now tied down by a small stitch at each intersection. Come up at A, and go down at B, as shown, until all threads are tied down. At the edge make a little half stitch if necessary (as shown).

Laid Work – Tied Diagonally[*]

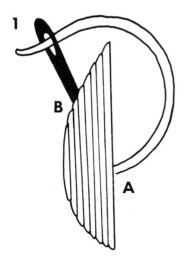

Having worked Laid Work over area (in direction shown), come up at A, down at B. This stitch lies across broadest area of the shape, to set the correct angle for the following stitches.

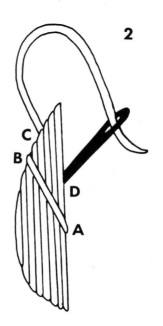

Come up at C, down at D, making a line parallel to A and B, about ¼″ above it. Then work from the center downwards until whole shape is laid with parallel slanting lines.

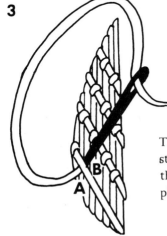

These lines must then be tied down with small stitches. Come up at A, down at B, going right through the material. These stitches should be placed alternately.

* Shaded Laid Work

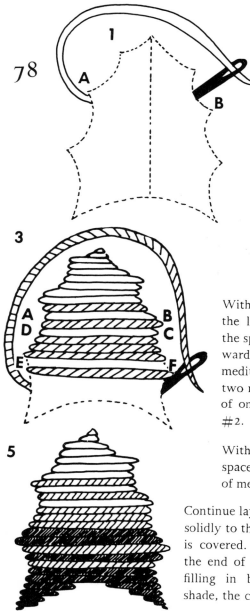

Come up at A, and go down at B. Use the lightest color and lay a line across the shape near the upper end at right angles to the center, (indicated here by dotted line). When the shape is irregular (as here), do not start at the tip, for the correct direction of the stitches may be lost by the time the broad part of the design is reached.

Working downwards, lay two *separate* lines the width of one thread apart, (as in diagram from C to D, E to F). Then working upwards, come up at G, down at H, and continue laying lines close together to the tip.

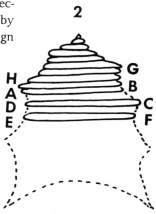

With medium color, fill in *between* the lines A-B, C-D, and E-F, where the spaces were left. Continue downwards, laying a solid block of medium-colored stitches. Then lay two more separate lines the distance of one thread apart (as shown) like #2.

With the darkest color fill in the spaces left between the separate lines of medium color.

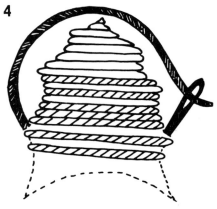

Continue laying dark-colored threads solidly to the bottom until the shape is covered. By spacing the lines at the end of each block of color and filling in between with the next shade, the colors blend softly.

Tie down with lines of Split Stitch. The direction of these lines depends on the shape of the design, but should be approximately at a 45° angle to the Laid Work lines.

In the case of this leaf, work a vein through the center first, then add the side veins in approximately parallel sweeping lines.

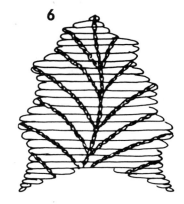

Burden Stitch *

This stitch may be used as a filling, or to cover large background spaces. It is attractive worked either very closely so that the basic threads hardly show, or quite wide apart to make an open lacy effect. It has the advantage of being an open filling, yet one where it is very easy to change color. The finished effect is almost like weaving. Generally it is best done in double thread, using the darkest color to underlay it and outlining the finished shape all round afterwards.

1

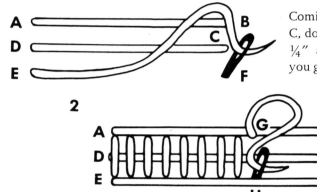

Coming up at A, going down at B, up at C, down at D, etc., lay parallel lines about ¼" apart (coming up the same side as you go down.)

2

Work the complete line (as shown), coming up at G and going down at H. G is immediately below and *really touching* line A-B; H is immediately above and *really touching* line E-F. Keep all stitches at right angles to the original laid lines.

3

Coming up at J, just below the line, go down at K, just above the line as in #2. Come up in between the previous stitches, fitting them in like bricks. Again take care to make stitches touch the lines above and below. The finished effect is like weaving, as though the vertical stitches disappear under the horizontal ones.

4

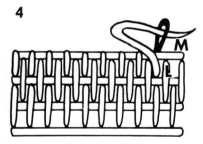

To finish the upper row, come up at L and go down at M, just over the top line. (It is easier to finish the top row of stitching after the scale has been set by the other rows.)

5

When shading use two needles and completely finish one row before going to the next. In row 3 for instance, work nearly to the center with light color, work one stitch of dark, change to light again and finish the row. In row 4 work the light stitches, then two stitches of dark and finish in light. (If all one color were worked first, insufficient space might be left for the other color, causing uneven spacing between stitches.)

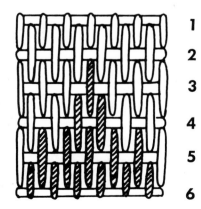

* Weaving Stitch

This is really exactly like sock darning! It may be done with at least two or three threads in both directions. Then when the weaving is completed evenly the result is a series of perfect squares in contrasting colors. It is also possible to use three or four threads for laying the first row of stitching, then to darn through with only one or two in the other direction. (This is useful to give a seeded effect on a strawberry, for instance.) Try to keep the outline even, for this stitch usually looks best if it is not outlined.

1

Come up at A, down at B, up at C, down at D, etc., laying threads side by side (the width of one thread apart).

2

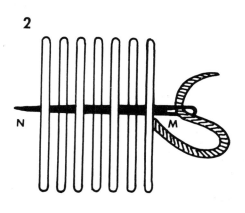

Change to a blunt tapestry needle, and using a contrasting color, come up at M. Weave under and over the threads, starting through the center (or the widest part). Go down through the material at N.

3

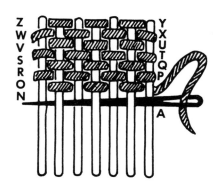

Come up through the material at O, and weave through the threads, go down at P, up at Q, continue to Z, pushing threads together so that even squares of each color are obtained. Go back to the center (A), and finish weaving the lower part.

Composite Stitches

So called because they are worked with more than one step and often more than one color.

82

Interlaced Cable Chain Stitch

This stitch is useful as a single line, or it may be worked in rows and interlaced to make a light open filling as shown. When used as the latter it is more effective to use double thread for the cable and single for the interlacing.

Work a Chain Stitch, coming up at A and going down again at A, holding the loop open – come up inside this loop at B and draw flat.

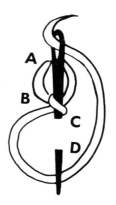

Holding the needle as shown, twist the thread once around it (as in French Knots).

Draw the twist tight and put the needle in at C, (outside the Chain Stitch loop). Now form another loop, and with the thread under the needle, come up at D and draw flat (as shown). This makes another Chain Stitch.

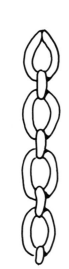

Repeat #2 again and continue making a Chain Stitch and a French Knot alternately so that the finished effect is like the diagram.

Using a blunt needle and a contrasting colored thread, lace the "cables" together (as shown). Do not draw the interlacing thread too tight.

Whipped Stem Stitch

Whipped Stem Stitch makes a fine smooth line stitch when the Stem Stitch is whipped with the same color. (The Stem Stitches should not be too long). An attractive candy cane effect is obtained if a contrasting color is used for the whipping. Generally it is best to use double thread in this case.

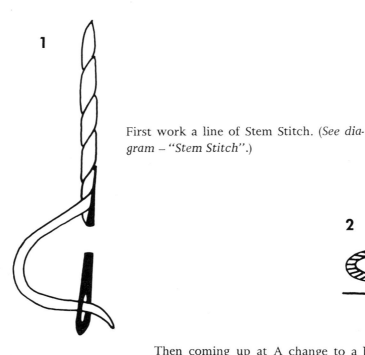

First work a line of Stem Stitch. (*See diagram – "Stem Stitch".*)

Then coming up at A change to a blunt tapestry needle and go through from B to C where stem stitches overlap one another. Pass only under the stitches, not through the material.

Continue, by repeating #2, until the whole line is whipped – finished effect should be like a raised cord.

Threaded Back Stitch

Work a line of Back Stitch, and using a blunt needle and contrasting color, thread it through as shown. The needle passes under the first Back Stitch from right to left (not into the material), through the second Back Stitch from left to right, and so on. Do not draw the interlacing thread too tightly or the effect will be lost.

Interlaced Running Stitch

With a heavy thread work a row of Running Stitches, then with a blunt needle and contrasting color, thread it through as in Threaded Back Stitch. Finally thread it back in the other direction, to make ovals of equal tension, as shown.

Interlaced Herringbone Stitch

First work a row of Herringbone. Beginning on the right, with a blunt needle and contrasting thread pick up the first bar of the Herringbone, slanting the needle downwards. Pick up the next bar slanting the needle upwards (direction of needle is indicated by arrows). Continue to the end of the line.

Threaded Herringbone Stitch

First work a row of Herringbone. With a blunt needle and contrasting color, pick up the under thread of the Herringbone cross, and weave along first the upper, then the lower edge in this way, as shown.

Tied Herringbone Stitch

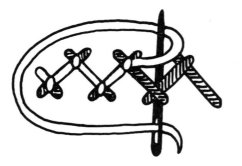

First work a line of plain Herringbone. With a blunt needle and contrasting thread, slide the needle under the Herringbone cross, pointing the needle towards the center of the line. While needle is held in position, twist thread over and under the needle, as shown. Draw tight to knot it. Work this Coral Knot on each cross along the line, always pointing the needle toward the center of the Herringbone band.

Detached Stitches

So called because each one is a small separate entity, which may be
used either as a "powdering" lightly scattered to fill an area, or solidly,
close together, or simply as a single isolated stitch.

Spider's Webs — Whipped and Woven

Both Whipped and Woven Spider's Webs should be worked very tightly in the center to show the spokes clearly, loosening the threads slightly toward the outer edge. The spokes may be covered completely and the Spider's Web outlined, or just the center may be worked, leaving the spokes showing all round. One or several colors may be used for each web, and one or more threads, depending on the size.

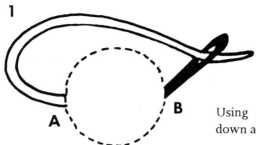

Using a blunt (tapestry) needle, come up at A, down at B, across center of circle.

Then come up at C, and down at D, (C to D should be slightly off center as shown). Come up at E, down at F, up at G and down at H. (H goes in quite close to D.)

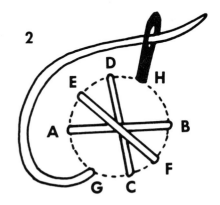

Spider's Webs – Whipped and Woven

This leaves a space for the needle to come up finally at I, a point midway between H and B. Then slide the needle under all the threads at their intersection. Take the thread and loop it across the needle and then under it as shown. Draw through and pull upwards to knot threads together in center.

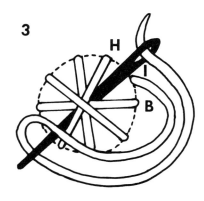

WHIPPED

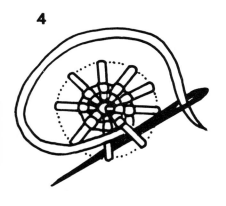

With the same thread, starting in the center, slide under 2 threads. Then place needle behind the thread just taken, slide under it, plus a new one. Progress in this way, back one and under two, till the spokes are all covered. Then either outline circle with Stem Stitch or leave plain.

WOVEN

Starting in center, weave under and over spokes, round and round, till whole circle is filled. Outline circle with Stem Stitch or leave plain.

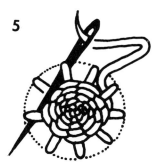

Raised Spider's Webs

Raised Spider's Webs should be small and may be either whipped or woven.

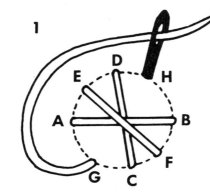

Using a blunt (tapestry) needle, come up at A, down at B, across center of circle.

Then come up at C, and down at D, (C to D should be slightly off center as shown.) Come up at E down at F, up at G, and down at H. (H goes in quite close to D.)

This leaves a space for the needle to come up finally at I, a point midway between H and B. Then slide the needle under all the threads at their intersection. Take the thread and loop it across the needle and then under it as shown. Draw through and pull upwards to knot threads together in center.

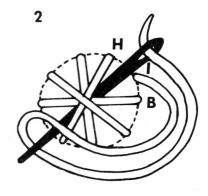

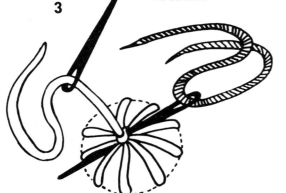

Pulling the knotting thread upwards, take another blunt needle threaded with any contrasting color and push it under all the spokes.

Unthread this needle and pull upwards with both strands of this contrasting thread, so that all the spokes are taut (as shown). Continue to hold it upwards while weaving round and round as in ordinary Woven Spider's Webs. Push in enough rows of this weaving so that the spider's web stands up in a point. Finally pull out the contrasting working thread, leaving the spider's web firmly raised.

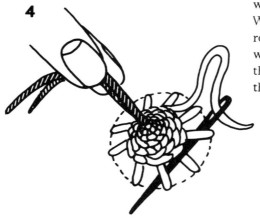

Bullion Knots

Double thread is usually best for this stitch. The knots may be used individually, or worked side by side. They should not be too long, or they will curl instead of lying flat on the material.

1

Bring needle up at A, go down at B, but do not pull thread through.

2

Stab needle up at A again but bring it only *halfway* through material.

Holding needle from below, twist thread round needle at A, until number of twists equals the distance between A and B.

3

4

Holding top of needle and threads firmly with finger and thumb of left hand, draw needle through with right hand, loosening coil of threads with left hand as you do so, to allow needle to pass through freely.

5

Then place needle against end of twist, at the same time pulling on the thread, as shown, until the knot lies flat on the material. If any "bumps" appear in the knot, flatten these by stroking the underneath of twist with the needle, at the same time pulling on the thread.

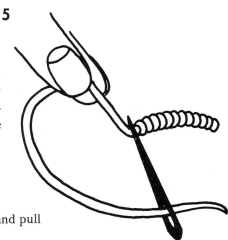

6

Put needle in close, at the end of the twist and pull through firmly.

Raised Needle Weaving

This is a good companion to Bullion Knots, but it has a slightly broader effect. It looks more attractive as a detached petal if it tapers at either end. Take care to draw the weaving thread very tight at both ends in order to bring this about.

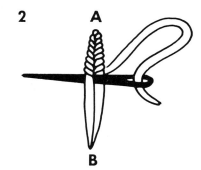

Using a blunt needle, come up at A, go down at B, and repeat, coming up at A, down at B again, so that two stitches lie side by side. Do not draw too tight.

Coming up at A once more, start to weave, (without going through the material). First pick up the left hand thread, pushing the needle through from right to left.

Then pick up the right hand thread, pushing the needle through from left to right. Continue till the two underlying threads are completely covered. From time to time pack the weaving threads together by pushing them up with the needle. Keep the tension even so that the line will be smooth.

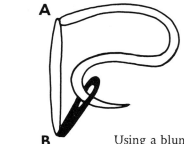

French Knots

French Knots may be scattered like seeding, to fill an area lightly, or they may be arranged in rows to fill a space solidly. The latter is most effective if each row is clearly defined and the knots lie evenly side by side. Alternatively they may be sprinkled closely but unevenly to produce an intentionally rough surface.

1

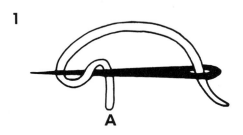

Bring needle up at A, twist thread once round needle as shown.

2

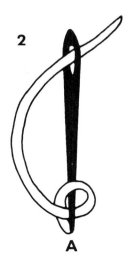

Put needle in at A, or just beside it, pull the thread until it fits *closely* round the needle (not too tightly). Pull needle through.

3

The finished knot. The thread should only be twisted once round the needle, as this makes a neat knot; *never* two or three times. The size of the knot is determined by the number of threads and size of the needle used.

Seeding

1

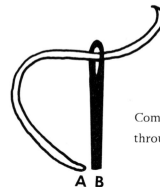

Come up at A, go down at B, a fraction away from A. Draw through, but not too tight.

2

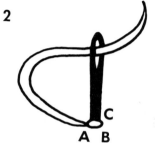

Coming up at A, work another stitch over the first. Go down at C close to, but not in the same hole as B. This makes the stitch fatter; the finished effect should be a raised knob, almost as broad as it is long.

3

Finished effect (enlarged). Work a series of these stitches all scattered over the surface in different directions. Take care not to pull the thread too tightly.

4

Finished effect showing shading stitches closely spaced at the edge, wider in the center.

Detached Chain Stitch

Make a single Chain Stitch and anchor it down with a small stitch (as at the end of a row of Chain Stitch). This stitch may be used as a filling, combined with cross bars, or scattered over the ground as a "powdering" like seeding.

Detached Twisted Chain

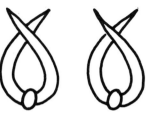

Come up at A, go down at B level with and to the left of A. Holding the thread across and then under the needle as shown, come up at C, in the center below A-B.

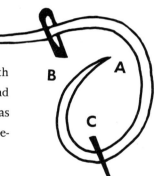

Anchor the stitch down outside the loop at D.

Finished effect.

Index of Stitches